What is sound?

1	What is sound?	2
2	Sound waves	4
3	How do we hear?	6
4	Hearing help	8
5	Making music	10
6	Wind instruments	12
7	Echolocation	14
8	Ultrasound	16
9	Sound in space	18
10	Sound is amazing!	20
	How is sound made? How is sound used?	22

Written by Emily Dodd

Collins

1 What is sound?

When a bee flaps its tiny wings, they move so fast they make a buzzing sound and the bee begins to fly. Another word for something flapping really fast is 'vibration'. All sounds are made when something vibrates.

When a lion roars, the vibrating parts are flaps inside its throat called vocal chords. These flaps are arranged in a square shape. The vocal cords wiggle up and down and from left to right to make a roar 25 times louder than a lawnmower!

You have vocal cords, too. Put your hand on your throat and say 'hello' – you should feel them vibrating.

2 Sound waves

Sound travels through the air in invisible waves.

That might seem strange, because you probably think of waves being something in the sea. In an ocean wave, the water moves up and down as the wave travels along.

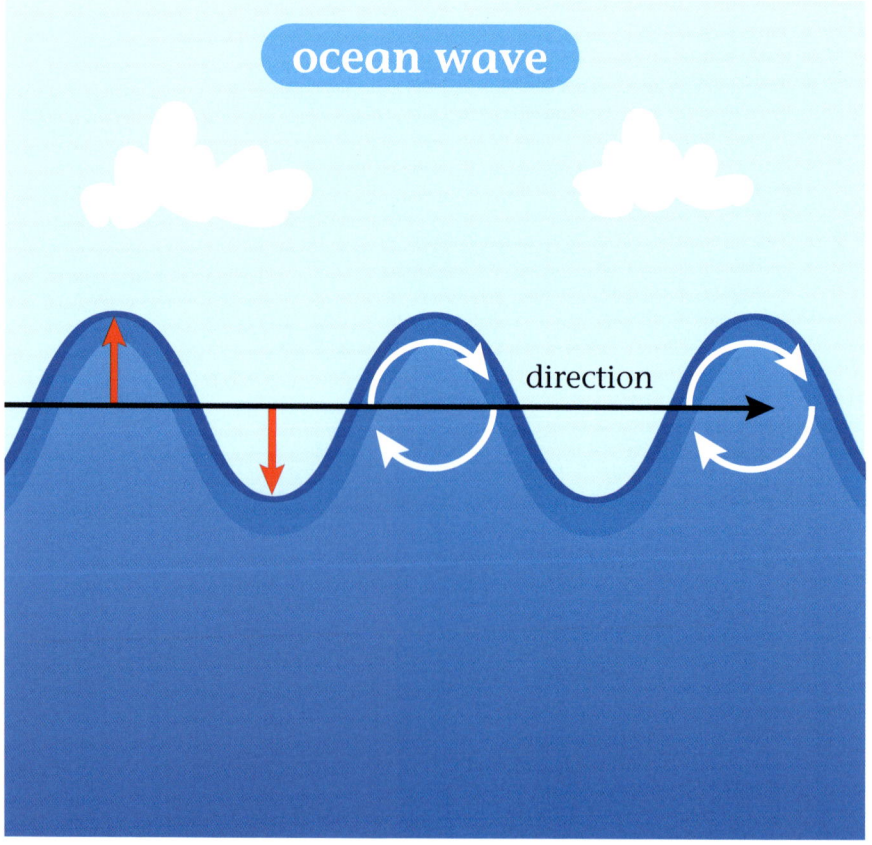

4

When a sound wave travels through the air, it travels differently to an ocean wave. It squashes and unsquashes the air in the direction it's travelling in.

Sound travels through the air in sound waves to get to your ears.

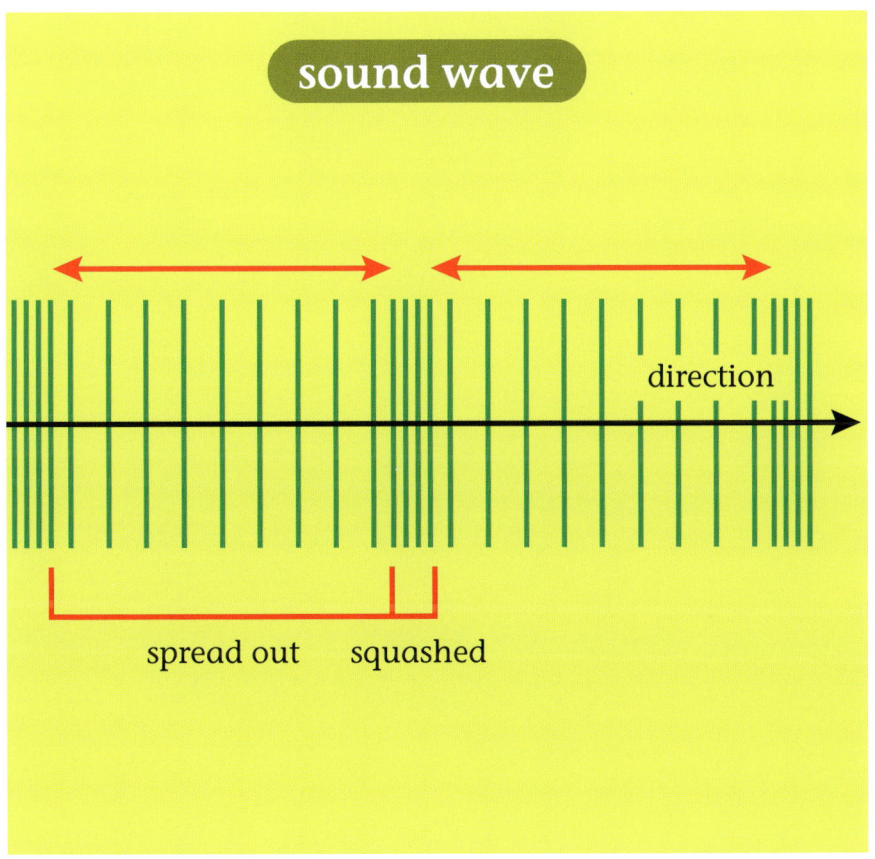

3 How do we hear?

Your ears are cups that collect sound. But there's much more to your ears, hidden inside your head.
Here's what happens when sound enters your ears ...

1 Ear drum
Sound waves hit a tiny drum, which vibrates, passing the sound on.

2 Hammer
The vibrations travel through a tiny bone called the hammer and on through two more little bones.

sound waves

3 Inner ear

These bones pass the vibrations into tubes of liquid. Tiny sensors pick up the vibrations and change them into an electrical signal.

4 Nerve

The electrical signal travels along a nerve to your brain where you process the sound.

4 Hearing help

When you can't hear sounds properly, it is called being deaf. Hearing aids are machines that take sounds and make them louder as they enter your ears. They can also filter out distracting background noises.

Sign language is a language that doesn't need sound. Instead, people move their hands to make words.

Some people hear sounds louder than others. A ticking clock can sound so loud that it's painful to hear. Ear plugs and noise cancelling headphones help to make sounds quieter and less distracting.

5 Making music

All musical instruments have a part that vibrates to make sound.

On a guitar, it is the strings – they vibrate when you pluck them.

Pressing the strings down against bars called frets changes the length of the strings.

fret

string

box

Changing the length of a string changes the speed it vibrates at. This also changes how high or low the sound is. The different sounds have letters to identify them, which are called 'musical notes'.

A guitar has a big wooden box that vibrates, along with the air inside it. This makes the sound louder. This is called 'amplification'.

6 Wind instruments

On a musical instrument called a recorder, you blow through a tube to make a musical note. When you place your fingers over different holes, it changes the length of the tube and the air vibrating inside. This changes the notes. A recorder is a type of flute.

The oldest flute ever discovered was made from the hollow bone of a cave bear. The remains are thought to be 80,000 years old! It had four holes in it and two of these are now worn away. Cave people would have used it to play music and to make animal sounds!

7 Echolocation

If you shout 'hello' in a cave, the sound waves sometimes bounce back off the curved walls. When this happens, you hear your 'hello' repeated back to you. This is called an 'echo'.

Bats make sounds as they fly. Their sounds bounce off objects and they hear the echo of their sound coming back. This helps them to know where things are even in the dark. It is called 'echolocation'. Bats also use it to hunt for insects!

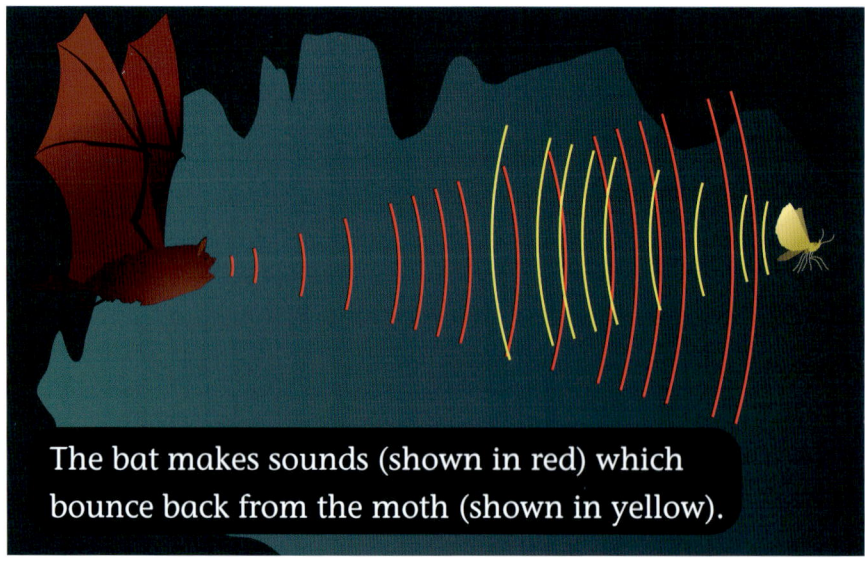

The bat makes sounds (shown in red) which bounce back from the moth (shown in yellow).

A machine called SONAR sends pulses of sound through the water and collects the echo to make a picture of things that are there beneath the surface.

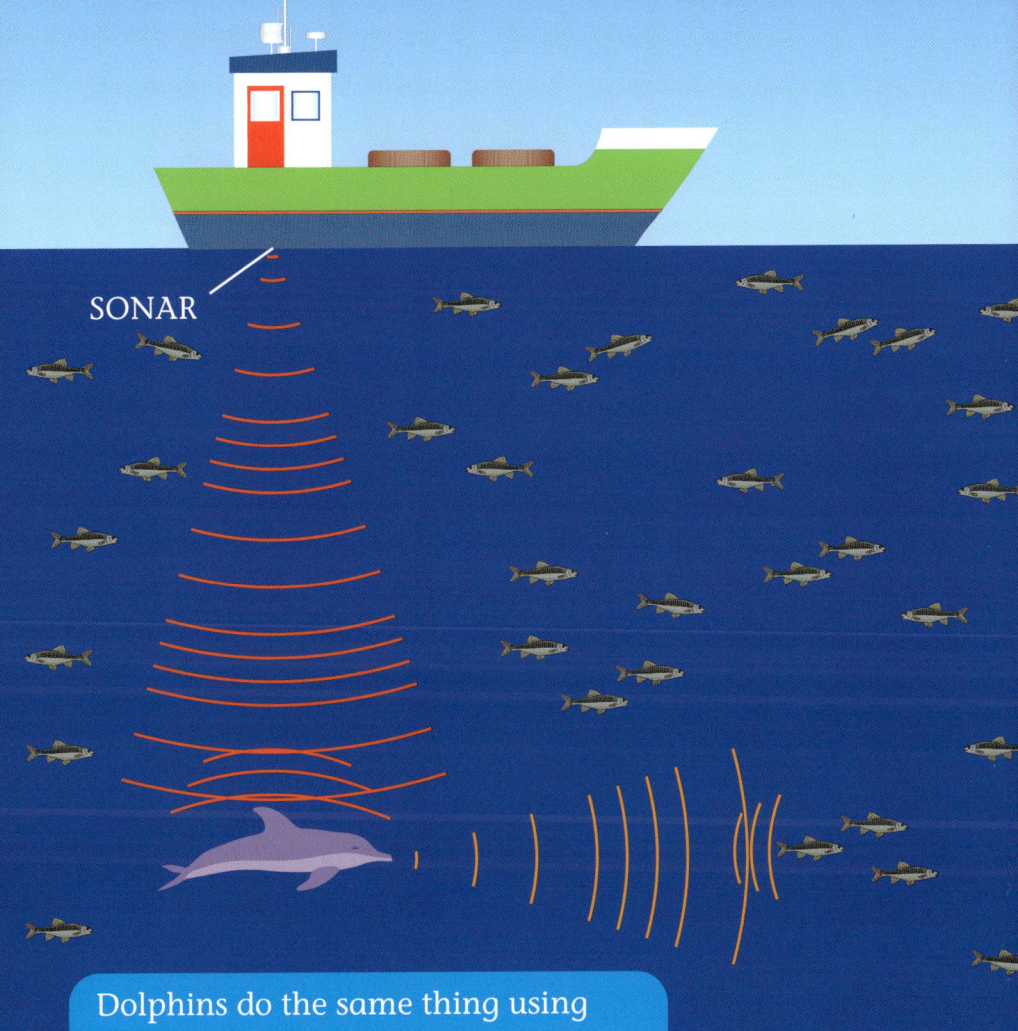

SONAR

Dolphins do the same thing using echolocation sounds to hunt for fish.

8 Ultrasound

Another invention that uses bouncing sound waves to see beneath the surface is an 'ultrasound'. This scanning machine makes sounds that are so high that human ears can't hear them. The sounds are very fast vibrations called ultrasound.

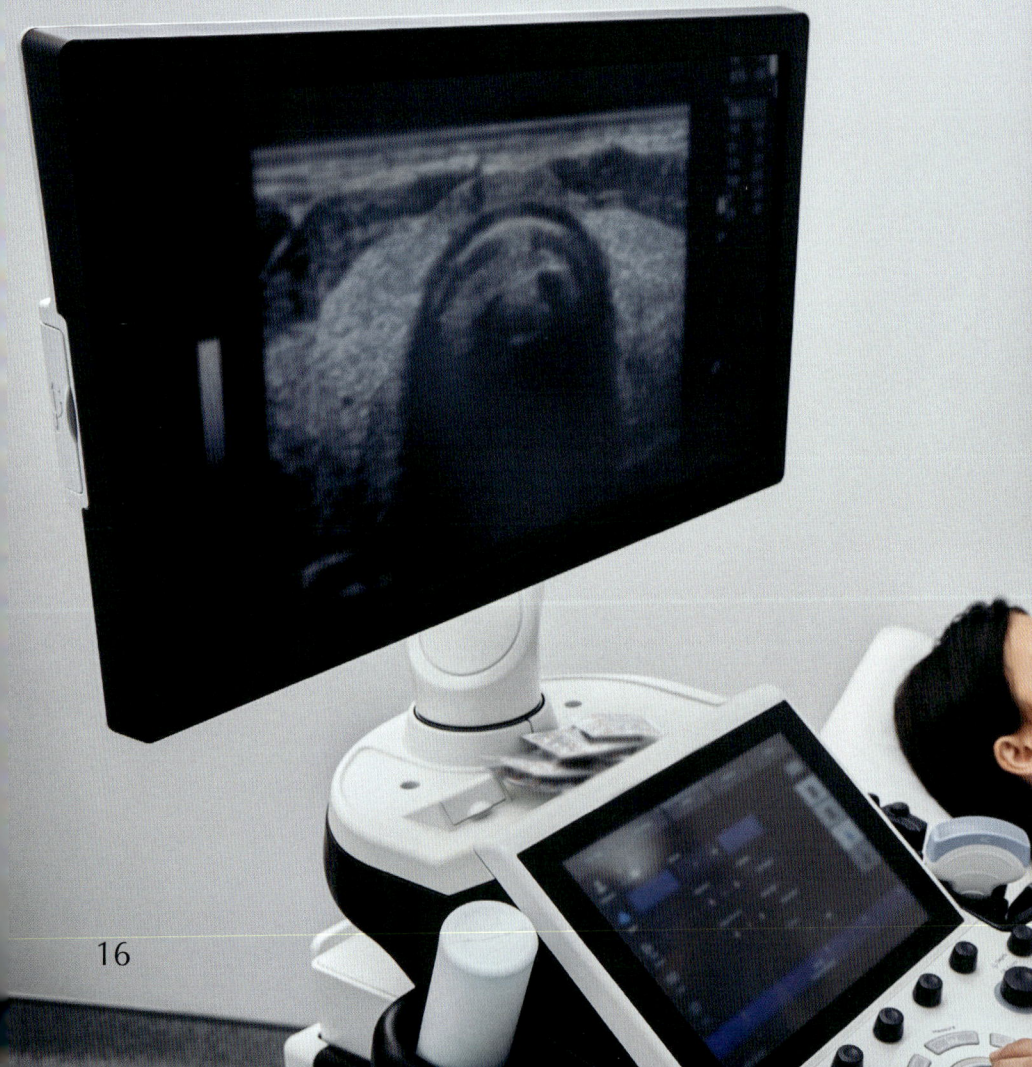

During an ultrasound scan, sound waves are sent through the body and they bounce back when they reach things. The ultrasound machine collects the echos and uses them to put together a picture of what's inside.

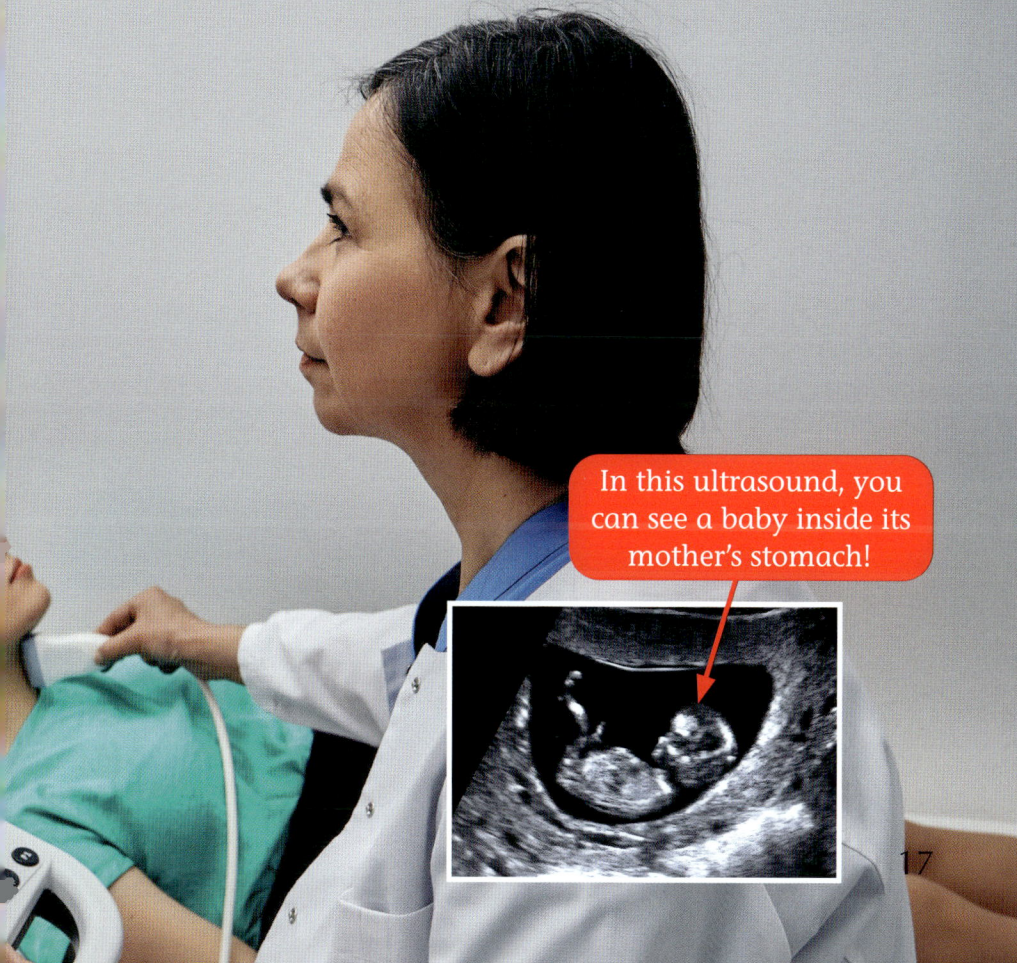

In this ultrasound, you can see a baby inside its mother's stomach!

9 Sound in space

In space, no one can hear you scream. You might think that's because there aren't many people, but it's actually because there isn't any air for the sound to travel through.

Air is all around you right now. It might seem like nothing, but if you blow up a balloon, you fill it with something – a gas called air. If you travel into space, you need to take air with you to breathe.

Sound waves vibrate through gases, liquids and solids but they stop when there is nothing to travel through. If there is no air, we call it a vacuum. Space is a vacuum, so sound waves can't travel through space.

10 Sound is amazing!

One of the reasons humans and animals make sounds is to communicate with each other.

We share stories and information to get to know each other. We call for the ball when we play football. We listen to instructions to learn. We laugh and we cry together.

When we watch a film or hear a favourite song, the sound waves travelling into our ears become something meaningful.

Sound helps us to know ourselves and each other, and to experience the wonderful world around us.

How is sound made?

How is sound used?

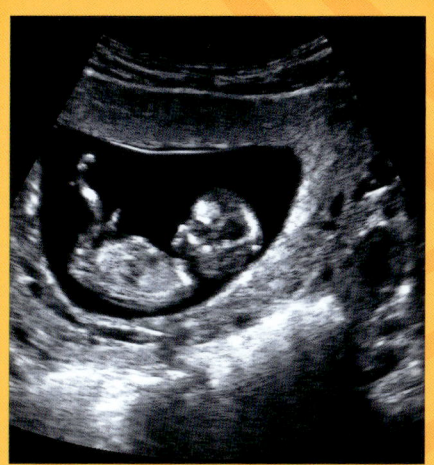
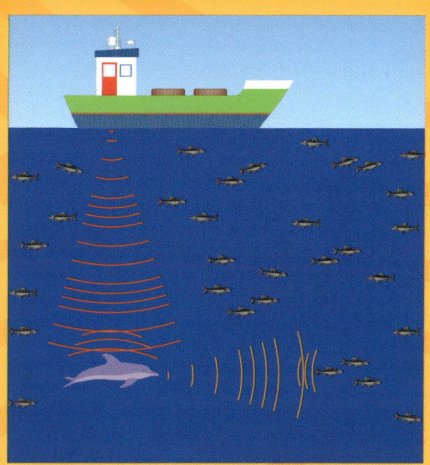

Ideas for reading

Written by Gill Matthews
Primary Literacy Consultant

Reading objectives:
- be introduced to non-fiction books that are structured in different ways
- answer and ask questions
- explain and discuss their understanding of books, poems and other material, both those that they listen to and those that they read for themselves

Spoken language objectives:
- use relevant strategies to build their vocabulary
- participate in discussions, presentations, performances, role play, improvisations and debates

Curriculum links: Science: Animals, including humans
Interest words: invisible, distracting, pluck, pulses, communicate
Word count: 1250

Build a context for reading
- Ask children to look at the front cover of the book and to read the title.
- Discuss the title, asking children what they think sound is.
- Read the back cover blurb. Point out that this is an information book. Ask children what they think they will find out from the book.

Understand and apply reading strategies
- Turn to pp2–3. Ask a few literal questions where the answers can be found on these pages, e.g. What does vibration mean? Where are your vocal chords?
- Talk to children about identifying key words in questions and scanning the page for those words.
- Allocate a chapter to each child. Ask them to read it and then to formulate a question that can be answered by reading that chapter.
- Give children the opportunity to ask each other their questions.